S0-CCJ-421

And the Message Is...

Ron Benson

Lynn Bryan

Wendy McDonell

Kim Newlove

Charolette Player

Liz Stenson

CONSULTANTS

Harold Fenlon

Ken MacInnis

Elizabeth Parchment

Annetta Probst

Prentice Hall Ginn Canada
Scarborough, Ontario

Contents

Bibliography

 Selections with this symbol are available on audio.

This symbol indicates student writing.

Canadian selections are marked with this symbol.

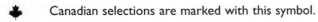

Hats

by Eric A. Kimmel
Illustrated by John Manthis

Many years ago a hatter named John Thomas opened a hat shop on Beacon Street. He painted an impressive sign and hung it above his door. The sign said:

> John Thomas, Hatter
> Fine Hats for Sale
> for Ready Money

A gentleman came walking down Beacon Street. He read the sign and shook his head. "Young man," he said, "your sign has too many words. No one has time to read them all. You should consider removing some."

"Which ones should I remove?" John Thomas asked.

The gentleman said, "You can take out the word 'Hatter.' Anyone who sells hats is obviously a hatter."

John Thomas got out his ladder. He climbed up to the sign and painted out the word "Hatter." Now the sign said:

John Thomas
Fine Hats for Sale
for Ready Money

Underneath was a picture of a hat.

An old woman came down Beacon Street. She stopped to read the sign. "Why does your sign say 'Fine Hats'?" she asked. "What other kind would you sell? You wouldn't be in business long if you sold hats of poor quality."

"You're right," John Thomas said. He climbed up the ladder and painted out the word "Fine." Now the sign said:

John Thomas
Hats for Sale
for Ready Money

Underneath was a picture of a hat.

As John Thomas climbed down the ladder, the wig-maker from the shop next door came out to read the sign. He shook his head and said, "Why does your sign say 'for Ready Money'? Everybody knows you sell hats for money. You don't trade them for vegetables."

John Thomas climbed back up the ladder and painted out the words "for Ready Money." Now the sign said:

John Thomas
Hats for Sale

Underneath was a picture of a hat.

Two sailors came ambling down Beacon Street on the way to the harbor. They looked up at the sign and laughed. "What a stupid sign!" one exclaimed. "It certainly is," said the other. "Of course he has hats for sale! Only a pumpkin head would think he gives them away."

After the sailors passed, John Thomas climbed down the ladder. Then he climbed back up and painted out the words "for Sale." Now the sign said:

John Thomas
Hats

Underneath was a picture of a hat.

Just before John Thomas closed his shop for the day, the minister from the church across the street came by. He said, "I have a suggestion to improve your sign. You don't need to include your name. All that interests people is what you're selling."

"You're right," said John Thomas. He got out the ladder, climbed up to the sign, and painted out the words "John Thomas." Now the sign said:

Hats

Underneath was a picture of a hat.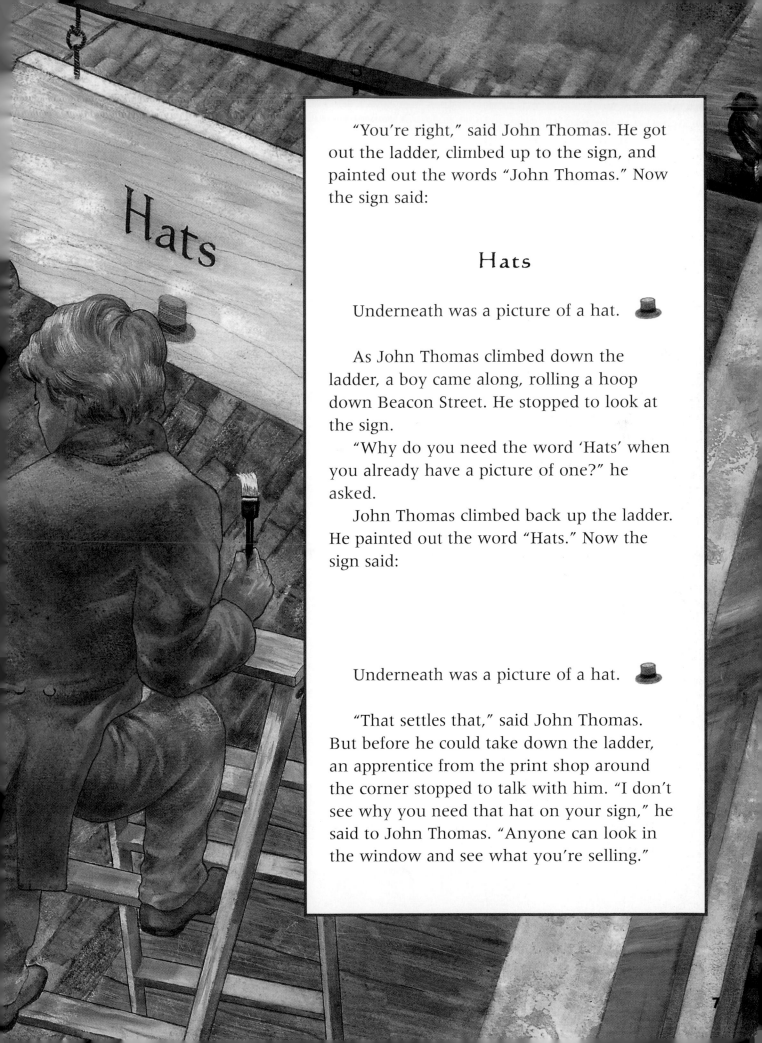

As John Thomas climbed down the ladder, a boy came along, rolling a hoop down Beacon Street. He stopped to look at the sign.

"Why do you need the word 'Hats' when you already have a picture of one?" he asked.

John Thomas climbed back up the ladder. He painted out the word "Hats." Now the sign said:

Underneath was a picture of a hat.

"That settles that," said John Thomas. But before he could take down the ladder, an apprentice from the print shop around the corner stopped to talk with him. "I don't see why you need that hat on your sign," he said to John Thomas. "Anyone can look in the window and see what you're selling."

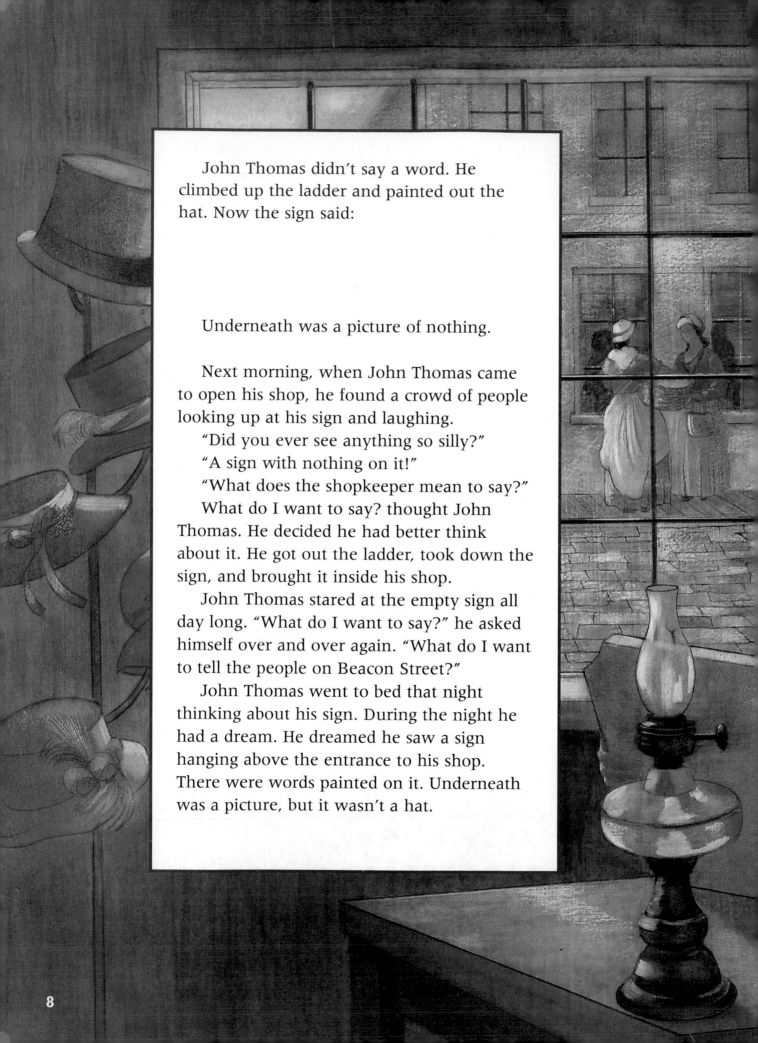

John Thomas didn't say a word. He climbed up the ladder and painted out the hat. Now the sign said:

Underneath was a picture of nothing.

Next morning, when John Thomas came to open his shop, he found a crowd of people looking up at his sign and laughing.

"Did you ever see anything so silly?"

"A sign with nothing on it!"

"What does the shopkeeper mean to say?"

What do I want to say? thought John Thomas. He decided he had better think about it. He got out the ladder, took down the sign, and brought it inside his shop.

John Thomas stared at the empty sign all day long. "What do I want to say?" he asked himself over and over again. "What do I want to tell the people on Beacon Street?"

John Thomas went to bed that night thinking about his sign. During the night he had a dream. He dreamed he saw a sign hanging above the entrance to his shop. There were words painted on it. Underneath was a picture, but it wasn't a hat.

John Thomas awoke from his dream. He jumped out of bed, got dressed, and hurried along Beacon Street to his shop. Once inside, he lit an oil lamp, got out his paints, and set to work on his sign. Now he knew what he really wanted to say.

John Thomas finished painting the sign just as the shops along Beacon Street began opening their doors. He got out his ladder and proudly hung the sign above the entrance to his shop. The people coming along Beacon Street stopped to admire the new sign gleaming in the morning light.

"Now there's a sign for you!"

"It says everything a good sign ought to say."

"Nothing more; nothing less," everyone agreed.

Painted on the sign was the bright face of the morning sun, shining in the sky over the city. And above it were these words written in gold letters:

Messages Everywhere:

A Communications Catalogue

Alphabet

A system of writing in which letters or symbols stand for the sounds of a language. There are about fifty different alphabets in the world. Hebrew, Greek, Persian, and Hindi are just some of the languages that have different alphabets from the one used in English. The English word "alphabet" comes from *alpha* and *beta*, the first two letters in the Greek language, yet English letters come from the Latin language. Now if that isn't mixed up, what is?

Bumper Sticker

An announcement that people stick on the bumper of a car. Some bumper stickers give simple information (*I Visited the Great Bat Cave!*). Others make personal statements or funny comments (*Honk If You Love Chocolate!*). No matter what your message is, this is a great way to announce it—as long as you don't mind being honked at.

CD-ROM

A computer disk made of melted glass beads that is used to store information. CD-ROMs can store pictures and music as well as text. CD-ROM stands for Compact Disk—Read Only Memory. When these disks were first made, you could "read" the information on them, but you couldn't erase or change it. Some new CD-ROMs are made so you can add information to them. Some CD-ROMs can store more words and images than a whole set of encyclopedias.

Desktop Publishing

Using a computer to combine text and images into a published piece. It's called desktop publishing because just one person sitting at a desk can do the work a whole team of writers, editors, artists, designers, and printers used to do. There are different kinds of *software*, or computer programs, to handle text, images, and page layout. You can even draw and paint using computer software. Desktop publishing lets you produce flyers, brochures, newsletters, and more.

E-Mail

Electronic messages people send to each others' computers. Through the Internet and other computer links, people can send e-mail all over the world quickly and cheaply. How quickly? Almost instantly. Computer users call regular mail "snail mail" because it's so slow.

Fax Machine

A machine that sends written messages and photographs through telephone lines. "Fax" is short for *facsimile*, which means "a copy." A fax machine turns a message or photo into electrical signals, which are sent over telephone lines. The machine at the other end turns the signal back into words and images and prints it out on paper. Many computers can send and receive fax messages right on-screen. Think of all the trees that saves!

Graffiti

Messages written or drawn on rocks or walls. The English word "graffiti" is borrowed from the Italian language and means *scribblings*. Some people just scribble their names and a date. Others draw pictures or write political messages. Still others write messages that are just plain rude. Graffiti may be fun for people who write them, but people who have to scrub them off walls think they're a real nuisance.

Hypertext Link

A way of moving from one piece of information on a computer screen to another piece of information. One place you find hypertext links is on the World Wide Web. Hypertext links are highlighted words or symbols on a computer screen page. When you click your mouse on the highlight, you get more information about that word. In fact, what you get is another page with still more highlights leading to still more information. The fun of using hypertext links is that if you keep clicking you never know where you'll end up!

Invitation

A message you send to invite people to an event. Invitations give exact information about what kind of event it is, and where and when it will take place. Many invitations have the letters RSVP on them. These letters stand for the French words *répondez s'il vous plaît,* which mean "please answer." This tells you that your host or hostess wants to know if you're going to come to the event or not. It's a good idea to answer, especially if you want to find any food left when you get there!

Journal A written record of your daily life and feelings. The English word "journal" comes from the French word *jour,* meaning "day." Some people do keep daily journals and write in them for years and years. If that sounds too heavy-duty, don't worry. When and what you write in your diary is strictly up to you!

Media The materials you use to do something. In art, paint or ink are examples of media. In public communications, the media include books, newspapers, magazines, movies, billboards, television, radio, and the Internet. The next time you want to see a movie or watch a hockey game on TV, just say you need to catch up on what's happening in the media.

Keypals Friends you write to by e-mail. (See **E-Mail**.) They're called keypals because you "key in" your messages to them by typing on a keyboard. People find keypals on special school computer networks such as Schoolnet, or in Internet interest groups. Do you believe in purple aliens from the planet Zog? Are you devoted to electric eels? There's probably someone out there who'd love to hear from you!

Network Equipment linked up to send messages. Radio and TV networks are groups of stations that usually carry the same programs. Computer networks link groups of computers so they can exchange information. A small computer network within a building or organization is called a LAN, for Local Area Network. The Internet is a large network of computers that covers the whole world. Why are networks called *net*works? Maybe because people use them to *fish* for information!

Letter A special kind of written message. A letter can be anything from a friendly note to a formal business message. It usually has a heading that tells who's sending the letter and who's receiving it, a *salutation*, or greeting, a *body*, or message, and a *closing* that says goodbye. If you're out of paper or don't have a stamp, just send your letter by e-mail. (See **E-Mail.**)

Optical Fibres

Thin strands of glass that carry messages. The messages are sent as flashes of laser light that zip through the fibres at high speed. The fibres are bundled together into optical cables that carry hundreds of thousands of messages at one time. Telephone companies have really lightened up!

Poster

A large illustrated advertisement that's *posted*, or stuck, on a wall or other surface. The most important part of the poster is the picture on it, and the words add only a few details. Have you ever heard the saying "a picture is worth a thousand words"? Posters prove it!

Quotation

An exact copy of someone else's spoken or written words. People use quotations to make their own words more interesting. It's fine to do this, but it's important to say whose words you are using. If you don't do that, you are *plagiarizing,* which means stealing someone else's words and pretending they are your own. Think how cross you'd be if someone did that to you!

Radio

A way of sending words and music through the air without wires. The words and music are transmitted as sound waves and picked up by a receiver in your radio set. I never listen to radio, you say? Oh, yes you do. Every time you use a cellular phone!

Satellite

A small object that circles around a larger object. *Communications satellites* are human-made machines that are launched into space to *relay,* or send back, telephone, television, and radio messages to earth. The messages are sent into space in the form of microwaves. High above the earth, the satellite picks up the microwave message and relays it to the right location on the ground. It's a bit like bouncing a ball off a wall!

Television

A way of transmitting sounds and pictures to distant places. In a television studio, sound waves and waves of light from images are turned into electrical waves and sent through the air. Far away, they're picked up by antennas or microwave receivers and changed back into waves of light and sound. Your television set gets these signals through an antenna or cable system. Television signals actually flow around us all the time. Wouldn't it be handy if we all had built-in antennas?

Ultimatum

Spoken or written words that mean "this is my final message." The English word comes from the Latin word *ultima,* meaning "the last." When your dad or mom says, "If you don't clean up your room, I'll cut off your allowance," that's an ultimatum. People sometimes give each other ultimatums when they quarrel. Nations do it before going to war. Ultimatums are messages that are not much fun to receive. It's also definitely safer not to send them!

Virtual Reality

A computer system that creates three-dimensional images. The word *virtual* means "not real, but just like real." Many virtual reality systems include a helmet and gloves. The helmet has a tiny TV screen in front of each eye. When you play a virtual reality game, a computer creates a picture and sends it to the helmet. What you see is a realistic-looking picture. The gloves have special devices called *sensors.* When you operate the game controls, the sensors tell the computer how to change the picture so you feel you're moving around and doing things. Someday soon you'll be able to shop and travel using virtual reality. Will it ever be as much fun as a trip to the mall or the beach? Who knows?

Website A location on the Internet service known as the World Wide Web. A website contains text, sound, and images that give information about a person or a company or some other organization. It also has hypertext links you can use to move to other locations on the Web. (See **Hypertext Link.**) About the only thing websites don't have is spiders!

Xerography A way of creating art by using photocopiers to copy objects. Artists can create all kinds of fascinating images using black-and-white or color copiers. Have you ever copied part of your hand by mistake while making a photocopy? Then you're already a xerographer!

Zero Part of the code used to run computers. Computers only understand two kinds of signals—whether an electrical current is switched on or off. Zero (0) stands for "off" and 1 stands for "on." Every piece of information your computer handles is coded as zeroes or ones. For example, the code for the letter "A" is 01000001, "B" is 01000010, "C" is 01000011, and so on. Imagine having to write out your homework that way!

Yahoo A search tool for finding addresses on the World Wide Web. (See **Website**.) Yahoo may sound silly, but it's really very useful. Just key in your subject, and Yahoo will tell you where to find information about it on the Web. You can find Yahoo's address in any printed Internet directory. Why is it called Yahoo? Maybe because that's what you yell when you find what you're looking for!

Fireflies

by Paul Fleischman

Illustrated by Philippe Béha

Light

Night
is our parchment

fireflies
flitting

fireflies
glimmering

glowing
Insect calligraphers
practising penmanship

Six-legged scribblers
of vanishing messages,

Fine artists in flight
adding dabs of light

Signing the June nights
as if they were paintings

flickering
fireflies
fireflies.

Light
is the ink we use
Night

We're
fireflies
flickering

flashing

fireflies
gleaming

Insect calligraphers

copying sentences
Six-legged scribblers

fleeting graffiti
Fine artists in flight

bright brush strokes
Signing the June nights
as if they were paintings
We're
fireflies
flickering
fireflies.

ABOUT THE

AUTHOR **PAUL FLEISCHMAN**

Paul Fleischman writes about many different topics, but all of his stories pay close attention to sound. In fact, this award-winning author's first love is music. Paul first learned the importance of sound in stories from his father, Sid, who also writes children's books. In high school, he spent hours in the library listening to Beethoven and Bach, learning how to shape his writing from what he heard. Before turning to writing full-time, Paul worked as a bagel baker and a bookstore clerk. He now lives in California with his wife and two children.

Dancing Bees

by Margery Facklam

Illustrated by Pat Stephens

When a honeybee discovers a rich supply of nectar, she flies back to the hive to tell the other bees exactly where the food is. The bee even tells them what kind it is and how good it is. How can an insect with a brain no bigger than a grass seed pass on all this information?

Dr. Karl von Frisch was the first person to find out. He put a dot of red dye on a worker bee that had found some flowers and watched as she returned to the hive. As he watched thousands of bees in this way, Dr. von Frisch figured out how they send their messages. They dance!

He called it the "waggle dance." The pattern of a bee's dance is a figure eight. She repeats it over and over again as her sister bees watch. The most important part of the dance is the straight run through the middle of the figure eight. That shows the direction from the hive to the food. If the bee is dancing outside the hive on a flat surface, she lines up with the sun, then turns to point toward the food. If the bee is inside, on the wall of the dark hive, her head points up, as if the sun were overhead. Then she turns right or left to show where the food is.

As she runs through the figure eight, the bee waggles her head and tail from side to side. The farther away the food is, the faster she dances. Different kinds of bees have different waggle signals. For German honeybees, one waggle

means the food is about fifty metres away. Italian bees, which beekeepers in the United States favor, use one waggle to mean about twenty-five metres.

As she dances, the bee's wings vibrate so fast that they buzz. The other worker bees touch the dancer with their antennae to feel the vibrations. They also sample a drop of the nectar she has found. In a few minutes, the first bees to figure out where the food is fly away. Then the others move up to touch the dancer, and they, too, leave the hive as soon as they know the directions. Before each bee flies off, she faces the sun, then turns the way the waggle dancer pointed during the straight run through the middle of the figure eight.

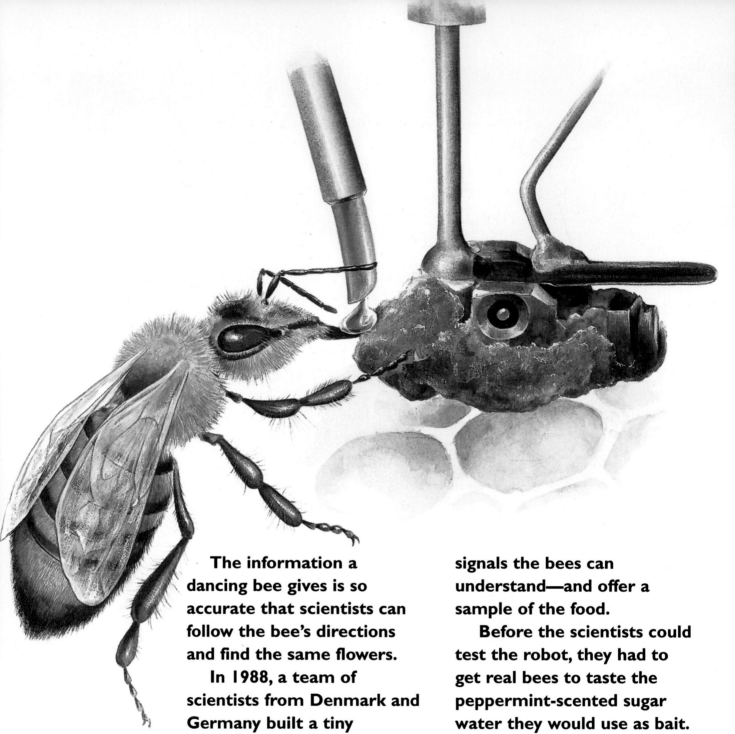

The information a dancing bee gives is so accurate that scientists can follow the bee's directions and find the same flowers.

In 1988, a team of scientists from Denmark and Germany built a tiny electronic robot honeybee that was run by a computer. The robot bee was designed to give a hive full of bees instructions to fly to a specific spot. The robot doesn't look much like a real bee, but it doesn't have to, because a beehive is dark. All the robot has to do is send signals the bees can understand—and offer a sample of the food.

Before the scientists could test the robot, they had to get real bees to taste the peppermint-scented sugar water they would use as bait. They put a dish of sugar water almost a kilometre and a half away from a hive and let a worker bee from that hive taste it. They had marked the worker bee so they could recognize her. When she flew back to the hive, she danced and gave samples of the food. Almost three hundred bees followed her instructions and found the sugar water.

The next step was to program the robot bee to dance the directions to the sugar water, which had been moved to a new spot. In the hive, the bees gathered around and paid attention to the robot bee. But could they follow the robot's directions? That was the big test. When the robot bee buzzed and waggled and gave samples of the food (the scientists released a drop of the sugar water through a tiny brass tube above the robot's head), almost a hundred bees found the sugar water. The robot wasn't quite as successful as the real bee, but the robot was obviously working.

Then the scientists tried some other experiments. For example, when the robot gave samples but didn't dance, only ten bees found the food. When the robot danced but didn't give samples, or when it danced and gave samples but didn't whir its wings, very few bees found their way to the sugar water. The scientists realized that the bees needed the whole message: the waggle dance, the whirring wings, and a taste of the food.

The keepers of the robot bee can hardly wait to find out what else it will tell them. They are ready for surprises.

ABOUT THE AUTHOR   MARGERY FACKLAM

Author Margery Facklam writes mostly about animals and nature because they are subjects that fascinate her. Before becoming a full-time writer, Margery was a curator at the Niagara Falls Aquarium and at the Buffalo Zoo. She even worked her way through college by taking care of a colony of porcupines! She says, "Writing is hard work, but it is exciting, fun, exasperating, and the most wonderful job in the world."

The Buzz of a Bee

The buzz of a bee,
The beauty of a tree,
The flight of a leaf,
The echoing of summer,
All make up fall.

Debra DeRulius
Age 9

Sounds of the Whale

Jeffry brought sounds of whales.
We talked about how beautiful
whales are.
They talk sad.

Clint Thorne
Age 9

Illustration by Janie Koitsis, age 9

Sounds

I like to hear
the sound of
the TV,
my Mother and
Father
talking to me
with kind words,
and birds singing.

Dzung Ha
Age 8

Messages

Messages
In envelopes carrying your name,
In the sky written in smoke,
In books that are full of
knowledge,
In codes that go under the sea,
Blimps in the air with messages,
Messages on the radio,
Messages carved in wood.

Messages
written and read
seen and heard
Messages

Ali Sultan
Age 10

When I wrote this poem I got inspired by my imagination and by the words I thought of. I'm proud of myself for writing this poem. It is special to me. It is part of me and my thoughts.

Ali Sultan

Satellite Report

Satellites flow around space in the earth's orbit. Satellites have a certain job — they get details out of space or the earth.

Satellites have been and will continue to be of great value to all people. Orbiting in the silent vacuum of outer space, satellites serve us on the ground by relaying our messages, by watching our atmosphere, by helping us locate and protect our resources, and by giving us clear glimpses of our universe.

Satellites are used directly or indirectly everyday. Many long-distance telephone calls travel through space via satellite without the parties on either side of the conversation being aware that it is happening.

Jeannie Kematch
Grade 8

Beyond Words

by Todd Mercer
Illustrated by Scot Ritchie

What if you needed to get a message to someone without writing or speaking. Could you do it? Believe it or not, people around the world communicate without words every day. Here are some ways they do it.

Codes and Symbols

The word *code* probably makes you think of sneaky spies and secret written messages. Not all codes are secret or even written, though. A code is any system of signals used to send a message. There are color codes and shape codes and codes in pictures. Picture codes are sometimes called *symbols*.

? Imagine you're a "snow bunny" who has just started skiing lessons. You're getting pretty bored with the beginners' hill and you'd like to try something a little more fun. You see a nifty-looking trail with no one on it. A sign with two black diamonds is right beside it. Should you try it out?

Many North American ski resorts use color and shape symbols to let skiers know how hard different trails are to ski.

Here are the four color symbols used to rate ski slopes:

 • A green circle signals the easiest slope.

 • A light blue square signals a difficult slope.

• A black diamond signals a very difficult slope.

• Two black diamonds signal an extremely difficult slope.

Not far away on that same ski hill, you might see a sign that looks like this:

It warns skiers of rocks under the snow. This sign works in two ways. Skiers know that a yellow diamond-shaped sign always means a warning about unusual conditions. The picture shows a skier breaking a ski on a rock. It's not hard to get that message!

Warning codes and symbols on household products work in similar ways. Reading and understanding them could save your life!

You're looking for something in the bathroom cupboard. There are a lot of containers in there, so you pull some out and put them on the counter. Then you knock one over and the cap comes off. Some stuff spills into the sink. Should you just wipe it up? Better take a look at that symbol first!

Many household products such as drain cleaners, cleaning liquids, and paint thinners contain strong chemicals. They can be very dangerous if not handled or stored properly. That's why Canada has a symbol system that alerts people to possible danger from these products.

The product symbol works in two ways—shape and image. For example, an eight-sided warning symbol means a product is more dangerous than a product with a three-sided warning symbol.

Caution　　**Warning**　　**Danger**

The symbol inside the frame tells you what the danger is. Here are the messages these symbols are supposed to send.

Corrosive: The product can burn your skin or eyes. If you swallow it, it will harm your throat or stomach.

Explosive: The container can explode if you heat it or puncture it. Flying pieces of metal or plastic from the container can cause serious injury, especially to your eyes.

Flammable: The product, or its vapors, will catch fire easily if it is placed near heat, flames, or sparks.

Poison: If you swallow, lick, or even, in some cases, breathe the chemical in, you could become very sick or die.

Hand Signals

Color and shape codes and symbols are great for sending general kinds of messages. They're not much help when people need to communicate directly with each other, though. Speaking and writing usually take care of that—but not if you're somewhere you can't speak or write!

Imagine you're a diver working in a team underwater. Maybe you're building something or cleaning up an oil spill. Your breathing tube gets caught on a sharp piece of metal and tears. You're too deep to make it to the surface in time. What do you do?

For safety reasons, all divers must dive in "buddy" teams of at least two people. All divers learn hand signals as part of their training. These signals can help save a diver's life. For example, the signal "Let's buddy breathe" might be used when you've lost your air supply. The signal tells your buddy, "I need to share air from your air tank."

Let's buddy breathe.

O.K.?

O.K.!

26

Not all hand signals are as simple as the ones used by divers. Deaf or hearing-impaired people can communicate using a special language of hand signals. The system is called American Sign Language (ASL), and the signs in it stand for words and ideas. Below are some ASL signs and what they mean.

| I | LOVE | YOU |

Some deaf or hearing impaired people use ASL to communicate with their hearing ear dogs. A hearing ear dog is trained to respond to the sounds within its owner's home, such as a phone ringing or a kettle boiling. The dog recognizes these sounds, jumps on its owner, and leads him or her to the sound.

Every hearing ear dog is given an ASL name and, over time, the dog learns to recognize its sign name and respond to it. Of course, all dogs need praise, and sometimes, correction. So the dogs also learn ASL signs for such terms as "good dog" and "bad dog."

Owners of hearing ear dogs use other hand signals too. The dogs are trained to respond to commands such as:

?

Imagine you're deaf or hearing impaired. You're supposed to keep an eye on your baby brother, but you get busy playing your favorite video game and forget. Suddenly Taffy, your hearing ear dog, runs into your room and jumps on you. You run across the hall and find the baby crying. How do you let Taffy know you're pleased with her?

Sit: snap of fingers

Down: point to the ground

Stay: American Sign Language signal for stay

Come: clapping of the hands

Bodies Talk Too!

Have you ever talked without moving your lips? Of course you have—by using movements and gestures. You raise your hand to ask a question in class. You nod your head for "yes," and shake it to mean "no." This kind of communication using gestures is called *body language.* It's so simple that everyone understands it, right? Unfortunately, it's not that easy.

You're waiting for a plane in a foreign airport and you're getting pretty bored. You spot a friendly-looking kid, so you go over and say, "Excuse me, do you speak English?" She nods her head. "Great!" you say. You open your mouth to say more, but she turns around and walks away. What happened?

Even simple body language doesn't always "translate" well everywhere in the world. That head nod that means "yes" in Canada means "no" in countries such as Turkey and Iran. In Bulgaria, a side-to-side head shake means "yes"!

Then there are gestures that have several different meanings in different parts of the world. Take a gesture called the *chin flick* for example.

If you did the chin flick in Naples, Italy, it would probably mean "No." Try that same flick in Belgium, France, or Tunisia and your message might more likely be "I couldn't care less." Do the chin flick in Greece and many people would think you're saying "I don't believe you." Travel west to Portugal and that same chin flick tells people "I don't know."

Now you know what to look for, it's easy to find more examples of communicating beyond words, isn't it? By the way, was that a nod, or a shake?

The Whispering Cloth: A Refugee's Story

by Pegi Deitz Shea
Illustrated by Stéphane Bourrelle
Stitched by You Yang

After Mai's cousins moved to America, Mai passed the days with Grandma at the Widows' Store, watching the women do *pa'ndau* story cloths.

She loved listening to the widows stitch and talk, stitch and talk—mostly about their lives back in Laos, and about their grandmothers' lives in China a hundred years ago.

All Mai could remember was life inside the refugee camp, where everyone seemed to come and go but her.

"Mai!" came Grandma's crackly voice. "Put Cousin's letter away. The words will disappear if you read them one more time. Come help me with the *pa'ndau* borders."

"But I don't know how."

Grandma threaded a needle and wrapped her hand around Mai's. "Push the needle up through the cloth," Grandma instructed. "And poke it back in when it has gone the length of a grain of rice."

For many weeks, Mai practised stitching, stitches that were short and straight, ones that looped inside others, ones that twirled into long strands, and stitches that looked like dots.

"Beautiful," praised Grandma, amazed at Mai's skill. "You are ready to go on."

Grandma then began drawing herbs and animals on the *pa'ndau* borders for Mai to embroider. By the end of the hot season, Mai was drawing and stitching her own border designs—vines of milky jasmine, bursts of purple orchid, palm trees plump with papaya.

"Hurry and finish, Mai," Grandma said one day. "The traders will be coming soon from Chiang Khan."

"How much will they pay for the ones I helped on?" Mai asked, knotting her last stitch.

"Twice as much as the others," Grandma bragged. "You sew even better than your mother did when she was alive. And her *pa'ndau* were prized throughout the hills."

"*Paang paang! Paang mahk!*" the traders complained when Grandma demanded 500 Thai *baht* for her *pa'ndau*. But when they saw the fine detail of the borders, the traders agreed to pay 400 *baht*—twice the usual price.

"Keep stitching, Mai," Grandma said when the traders left. "And we'll fly from this camp before the rabbit breeds again."

Mai's hands went back to work on the borders. But her eyes and ears were drawn to the tribal stories the women stitched *inside* the borders. Every time the wind rippled the *pa'ndau* hanging at the Widows' Store, Mai heard words in the air.

"Grandma, I want to do a whole *pa'ndau* myself," she said finally. "Can you give me a story?"

"If you do not have a story of your own, you are not ready to do a *pa'ndau.*"

Mai tried for days to think of a story she could stitch. But all the good ones were already whispering around her.

One night, Mai's fingers cramped so much that she couldn't sleep. Grandma lay down on the mat beside Mai, enfolded her, and rubbed her hands.

Grandma's soothing made Mai remember how she had slept when she was little, snug as a banana in a bunch. Snug...with her mother behind her, her father in front of her. Mai's lower lip began to quiver.

"I want my mommy and daddy," she cried softly.

"I know, I know...," Grandma said. "Call to them, Mai. Call their spirits with the words in your fingers."

Mai closed her eyes and tried to picture her parents. Flashes, noises, smells bombarded her. A story was erupting in her head—a story she could stitch....

Little Mai slept between her mother and father, who were very beautiful even though blood dripped from their heads.

Grandmother put Mai in a basket on her back and ran through the paddies to the riverboats.

Soldiers fired. Bullets whistled over the people's heads and made rings in the brown Mekong.

On the other side of the river, soldiers in different clothes took them to a crowded village inside a tall fence.

People stood in long lines to get little bags of rice and dried fish. Mai grew taller. She passed the days watching the blacksmiths make knives and tools. Sometimes she pounded balls of silver into flat sheets for the jewellery maker.

She helped Grandmother grow chilies and coriander.

Mai searched for empty glass bottles. When she put them upside down in the ground around her hut, they sparkled.

This is how Mai lived for many years.

Mai finished her *pa'ndau* as the rainy season was ending. "Grandma, how much will the traders pay for my *pa'ndau*? Enough to fly to America?"

Grandma ran her fingers over the needlework. Then she took the *pa'ndau* by the corners and held it up to the breeze. She turned her head so that her good ear grazed the stitches.

After a long time she whispered, "The traders will offer nothing."

"Nothing?" Mai cried in frustration.

"The *pa'ndau* tells me it has not finished its story," Grandma replied.

"But I have nothing left to tell."

Grandma squinted, pushing yellow through the eye of a needle. "There is always more thread."

Mai grabbed her *pa'ndau* and ran through the muddy lanes of brown huts all the way to the camp border.

There, rainwater gushed freely through the barbed fence and joined a stream beyond.

Mai stood in the water and let it wash over her feet. She stared out past the fence for a long time. Then she sat down on the bank and began to stitch.

33

One day, Grandmother and Mai flew inside an airplane. They glided softly above boxes of land to a village where homes were big as mahogany trees.

Mai and her cousins built men with white crystals, swam in curling salt water, read books with beautiful pictures.

And at night, Mai snuggled with Grandmother in a yellow bed with a silky roof.

Many days later Mai rejoined the women at the Widows' Store and showed them her finished *pa'ndau*.

"It is very fine," Grandma said. "I like the bed with the roof."

"How much will the traders give me?"

"It is worth much....What do you think?"

Mai picked up the *pa'ndau*, but the wind blew it back against her. The short, rough stitches of her father's hand stood up from the cloth

to stroke Mai's chin. She tried to speak, but the smooth
stitches of her mother's cheeks hushed her lips.

"Mai?" Grandma nudged her. "How much?"

"Nothing," Mai whispered, clutching the story cloth.

"Nothing?"

"The *pa'ndau* tells me it is not for sale."

Glossary

Baht (*bot*) is Thai money. One *baht* equals about 5 cents. The traders paid 400 *baht*—about 20 dollars—for Grandma's *pa'ndau*. Such *pa'ndau* now sell in North America for at least $50.

Hmong (*mung*) people originated in the mountains of Southwest China more than four thousand years ago and have populated the hills of northern Vietnam, Laos, and Thailand. Over two hundred thousand Hmong refugees now live in North America.

The **Mekong River** (*MAY kong*) originates in Southwest China, courses south through Laos, and forms a long length of the border between Laos and Thailand. It continues south through Cambodia and Vietnam and empties into the South China Sea. Communist soldiers in Laos regularly ambushed Hmong refugees who tried to cross the Mekong to Thailand.

Paang Mahk (*pang*) means "expensive," and (*mock*) means "too" or "very" in the Thai language. In Thailand, people negotiate the cost of most foods and services.

Pa'ndau (*pah NOW*) means "flowery cloth" in Mai's Hmong language. It is an embroidered tapestry that may include traditional patterns, images of wildlife and plants, or a story. In North America, quilting is a similar folk art.

ABOUT THE AUTHOR PEGI DEITZ SHEA

Author Pegi Deitz Shea first thought of the idea for this story when she visited the Ban Vinai refugee camp in Thailand. There, as she watched women stitching *pa'ndau* at the Widows' Store, she saw a young Hmong girl, who became Mai in *The Whispering Cloth*. Pegi is also the author of *Bungalow Fungalow*, and has her own public relations business. She lives in Rockville, Connecticut, with her husband and their two children.

The Painting

by John O'Brien
Illustrated by Kasia Charko

I think Mrs. Spencer was about eighty—maybe even older. Her hair was thin and white, and her face was full of wrinkles. She limped slightly.

She lived next door, all alone, and Mom was always saying to us: "Go and visit her. Go and say hello. She likes to see young ones around."

"But, Mom," Cathy and Peter would say. "We don't need to. Robert's *always* there. He just about lives there."

My face would turn red.

"Don't tease him," Mom would say. "It's kind of Robert to visit her. She likes to see him. She tells me he's a real gentleman."

"A gentleman!" They thought this was a great joke. "A gentleman!"

I was embarrassed but never said anything. It was true that I visited Mrs. Spencer quite often. Sometimes I would spend half of Saturday morning at her old place. I wasn't trying to be kind. I enjoyed visiting her. She was an artist, and I wanted to be an artist, too, one day. Sometimes I would show her paintings or drawings I had done at school.

"Lovely," she'd say. "Just lovely." And then she would share some secret about making paintings and drawings even better.

"Mrs. Spencer, what do you do with all your paintings?" I asked one day. "You must have done hundreds and hundreds of them."

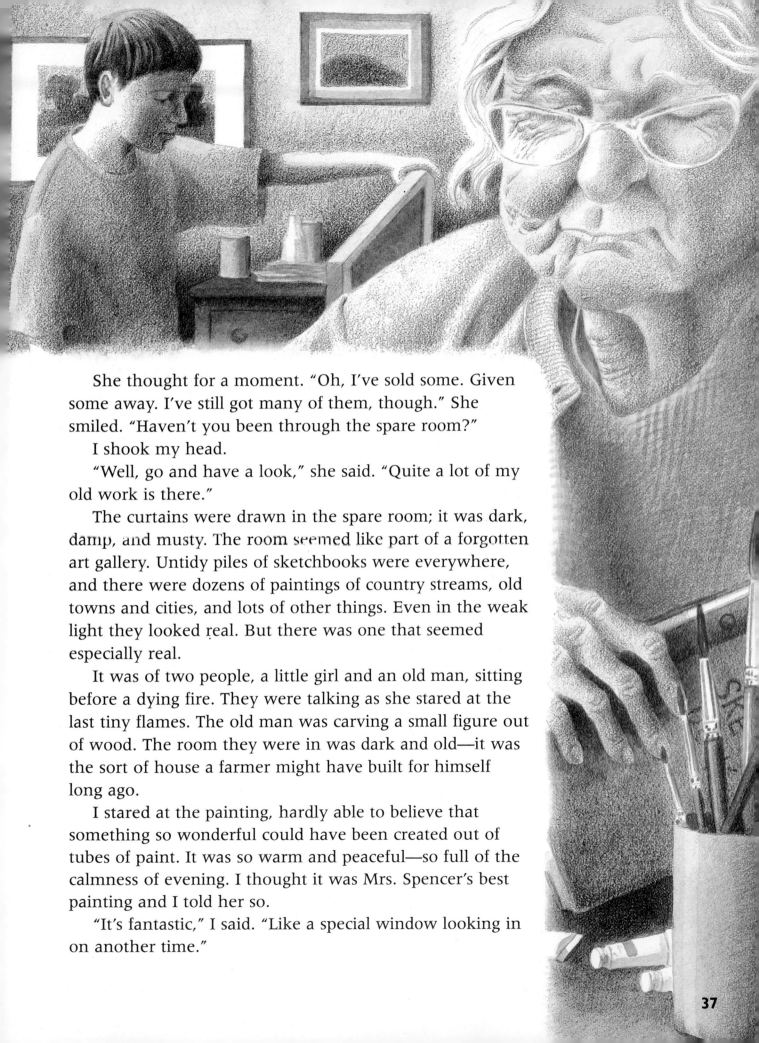

She thought for a moment. "Oh, I've sold some. Given some away. I've still got many of them, though." She smiled. "Haven't you been through the spare room?"

I shook my head.

"Well, go and have a look," she said. "Quite a lot of my old work is there."

The curtains were drawn in the spare room; it was dark, damp, and musty. The room seemed like part of a forgotten art gallery. Untidy piles of sketchbooks were everywhere, and there were dozens of paintings of country streams, old towns and cities, and lots of other things. Even in the weak light they looked real. But there was one that seemed especially real.

It was of two people, a little girl and an old man, sitting before a dying fire. They were talking as she stared at the last tiny flames. The old man was carving a small figure out of wood. The room they were in was dark and old—it was the sort of house a farmer might have built for himself long ago.

I stared at the painting, hardly able to believe that something so wonderful could have been created out of tubes of paint. It was so warm and peaceful—so full of the calmness of evening. I thought it was Mrs. Spencer's best painting and I told her so.

"It's fantastic," I said. "Like a special window looking in on another time."

Mrs. Spencer was pleased. "I've not done many like it," she said. "Sometimes it seems alive, that one."

I knew what she meant. One day I hoped to do a painting that seemed alive.

I went back to Mrs. Spencer's the following Saturday. I watched her paint for several minutes, then said, "Can I have another look through your spare room, Mrs. Spencer?"

"Of course, Robert," she said. "Any time you want."

I hurried straight to the room and then straight to the painting. I sighed with delight. It seemed even better than before. This time, I noticed more detail—old mugs hanging on the wall, curls of wood on the edge of a bench, golden leaves on a tree outside the window.

It was strange, though; the painting seemed brighter than it had the first time. The fire in it had all but died away—nothing was left of it but a few glowing coals. The brightness was coming *through* the window, as if the weather outside had improved.

"Mrs. Spencer," I said a little while later, "do you find that paintings sometimes seem to change?"

"Oh, yes, dear," she said. "Why, sometimes I love a painting one day but really dislike it the next. Paintings are funny like that."

A few days later a storm blew up from the south. The temperature dropped and dropped, and Mom worried about Mrs. Spencer.

"She doesn't eat well," she said. "Not well enough for this sort of weather."

"We've got plenty of this stew," said Cathy. "Send some of it over with Robert."

Mom nodded. "Yes, I think I might. You wouldn't mind, Robert, would you?"

So I ran over to Mrs. Spencer's, carrying a well-wrapped-up bowl of stew. She let me in at once. I went into her cold, cold lounge while she got a spoon.

"Why did you let your fire go out?" I called. "It's freezing in here."

"Has it gone out?" Mrs. Spencer called back. "I didn't notice."

Just like her, I thought. When she was working, she never noticed anything. I hurried out to her shed and collected a pile of wood. Soon I had a roaring fire going, and Mrs. Spencer sat near it, eating her stew.

"This is wonderful," she said. "Do thank your mother." She smiled at me. "And thank you, Robert, especially for the fire. I hadn't realized just how cold it had got."

Before I left the house, I decided to have another look at the strange painting in the spare room.

It'll be just as it was before, I told myself as I slipped up the dark hallway. It's a painting, not a living thing. It can't really change.

But it had.

The fire in it had grown from a few glowing coals into a huge crackling blaze. And on the side of the bench, where I couldn't possibly have missed it before, was a steaming hot bowl of stew, just waiting for the old man to eat it.

Backing away, I fell over a pile of paintings. I rushed from the room and flew out of the house as quickly as I could. I didn't stop running until I was safely home again, in the kitchen with all the others. And my heart didn't stop pounding until long after that.

The next evening, Mom wanted me to go back to Mrs. Spencer's with a small pot of hot soup. I wasn't very happy. I wanted to keep away from her place, but it wasn't something I could explain to Mom or the others.

"Oh, all right," I said. I picked up the pot and hurried outside into the icy wind. I would keep well away from the horrible living painting in the spare room, anyway.

But Mrs. Spencer had moved the painting into the lounge. It was facing the doorway, staring at me, as I entered the room.

"See, Robert," she said. "Your favorite."

I nodded, and slowly backed out into the kitchen. "I've got to get going," I whispered.

"Wait a minute, Robert," said Mrs. Spencer. "Have another look at the painting before you go. How does it seem to you now?"

I stared at it through the wide doorway. "The fire in it has grown," I said in a small voice. "It's grown quite a lot. And it shouldn't have."

"Perhaps you're right," said Mrs. Spencer, studying the painting. "Perhaps it is too much." And she collected several brushes and a pallet off the table and stroked dark paint around some of the larger flames.

I watched her, open-mouthed. "Mrs. Spencer," I cried. "I thought you finished that painting ages ago. I thought it was an *old* one."

Mrs. Spencer chuckled. "Oh, no," she said. "It's barely a year old. And I often touch it up. In fact, if I didn't leave it in the spare room, I'd probably be working on it every day."

"But why?" I asked.

"Often when I look at it I just feel it wants to change," she said. "I'm not quite sure why."

"Who is it?"

"Oh, it's my old grandfather," she said. "Back when I was younger than you are now. For years I've tried to paint him like that, by the fire. It's where I remember him most. But this is the first one I've done, where I feel he's really there."

"Is that why it seems alive?" I asked.

Mrs. Spencer looked at me strangely for a moment and then nodded. "I might be able to leave it for a while, now," she said. "But come spring, sparkling sunshine will be aching to flood inside and freshen up that dark, wintry room." She smiled at me. "Just wait until you see it in spring."

I looked at the painting once more, for quite a long time. It seemed perfect, but I felt sure that it would seem even more perfect in the spring.

Messages in Paintings

Untitled

T he sea and sky are full of mysteries, and children at play pause to wonder. Where do the ships come from? Where do they go? And the animals that hide in the clouds? What stories could they tell of what happened upon these shores long ago?

by Warabé Aska

Give Thanks to the Grandmothers

I have a fear of mountains. I'm scared of closed-in spaces like those spaces in between the mountains, because I grew up on the plains where it's flat.

When I first came to Vancouver, I had to drive through the mountains for twelve hours. My understanding cousin accompanied me on the trip. After we made it to our destination, my cousin said, "Give thanks to the Grandmothers for our safe passage." I have learned about respecting the Grandmothers and Grandfathers, the ancestors who have gone on to the Spirit World. I have learned that I can pray to them and that they will help guide me, just as the Creator does. My Great-Grandmother, Peggy Louis Natuasis, stands third from the left.

by George Littlechild

Plowing

Plowing was a long, lonely job. On the old tractor William didn't fall asleep so easily because its steel wheels made for a rough ride. But the new tractor had rubber tires and there was only the noise of its two cylinders to keep him awake. "Bach, bach—bach, bach" its exhaust repeated over and over all day long and even after supper till it was completely dark. As long as William could still make out the furrow he had to keep plowing.

Making turns on the tractor was easy enough after the first year of bungling. William also got the knack of pulling the trip rope to raise the plow when he reached the end of a furrow or to drop it after making the "E" turn. A flock of gulls followed him as he plowed to gobble up the worms and bugs the plow turned up.

by William Kurelek

44

Supper Table

his was our supper table back in 1968, when our oldest child was ten. Simple and honest, it was not "set up." It sat jumbled and untidy in its pool of autumn light. It told a lot about us.

by Mary Pratt

Student Writing

Aganetha

There was an artist in the school, her name was Aganetha Dyck. She arrived here April second and she left April the sixth. It was fun. We painted and made all kinds of things. On the sixth of April we had a big show. Lots of people came. There was a reporter from Interlake Newspaper who did an article about Aganetha and our art work. Dawn Brown made a cake for Aganetha. She was very happy. I hope she comes back soon.

Kendra Mowatt
Grade 7

Sandman

A dolphin, a shark,
a seal or a whale,
a cloud, the sun,
or even the moon.
A monster, a horror,
sometimes a goon!

I said to my mom,
"It all seems real."
"It's just a dream,"
she said, "not a big deal."

And as I get sleepy,
and start dreaming again
I sigh,
and the sandman
drops sand in my eye.

Kara Evelyn
Age 10

The Quilt

To me, a house is a warm and safe place. A house is welcoming and respectful at the same time. A house is strong but gentle and sensitive. That's why I picked a house for my square of the quilt.

Ruth Gallivan-Smith
Age 11

The square Ruth Gallivan-Smith made for the quilt made by her class.

When I am alone at night trying to go to sleep and I can't, I say a poem to myself, and at school I write them down in my journal. This particular one was one of my favorites. Because my Mom told me about the sandman when I was about seven, I wrote about him in a poem and this one is it. I started writing when I was 6 years old.

Kara Evelyn

Eagle Feather— An Honor

by Ferguson Plain

I remember when Mishoomis and I would go for walks in the bush, Mishoomis would tell me stories of when he was a little boy and legends that his father told him.

As we would walk in the bush, Mishoomis would show me what plants were alright to eat and what was good medicine and what was bad.

Mishoomis could speak English and Ojibwe, but spoke mostly Ojibwe, especially when he had tea with Nookomis.

One day Mishoomis and I were walking through the bush. It was just after winter, and Mishoomis would stop and observe his surroundings, looking at every plant, bud, and tree. Then with a gentle smile, he would say, "Wii aabawaa. Everything shows its life."

I liked spring and summer with Mishoomis the best because he would take me camping in the bush and we would make a fire. Then Mishoomis would beat his drum softly and chant songs in Ojibwe.

I remember once when Mishoomis and I were sitting along this creek, he said to me, "Nooshehn, there will be a time when you will receive the highest honor that is given to an Anishinabe."

So I asked him what that was and he said, "An

eagle feather." Mishoomis also said that I must do good deeds for my people or my clan.

"How do I do these deeds?" I asked him.

"Let your heart guide you, Nooshehn," he said.

It was almost three months since Mishoomis and I walked in the bush together. But I would go visit with him at his bedside every day and we would talk of when we walked through the bush and the things we would find. Then Mishoomis would tell his legends and stories of the old days and I would sit and listen.

Nookomis finished my traditional outfit to wear when I danced in the summer Powwows. She had worked on it all winter. But I knew it wouldn't be much fun this year because Mishoomis was sick, and we always danced together.

One day Mishoomis told me that he would not be able to dance with me at the Powwow this year. He said the Great Spirit would soon be sending an owl for him and he would join Mother Earth.

The day of our traditional Powwow came and Mishoomis was still ill, so I wanted to stay with him at his bedside. But Nookomis and probably Mishoomis would have been upset if I didn't dance this year, so I went.

As I was going through grand entry all I thought about was walking through the bush with Mishoomis and the fun we had camping, talking and finding things there. But my heart was sad knowing he was ill and still in bed.

After the snake dance the chief called me up to the grandstand as he announced that I was to receive an Eagle Feather that Mishoomis was giving to me.

As the chief placed the Eagle Feather on my roach the drummers started chanting and I had to dance around the grandstand on my own first and then with my family and friends.

After the ceremony was over I rushed back to see

Mishoomis to ask him why I had received his Eagle Feather. I sat beside him, excited and confused. Mishoomis asked me why I had a puzzled look on my face and I told him that I didn't understand why I had received his Eagle Feather.

Mishoomis placed his hand on my shoulder and told me that I had achieved a good deed from the first day he held me, as a baby, in his arms. "You are my Nooshehn and I could not have asked for anything more," he said.

To this day as I walk through the bush I can still hear Mishoomis telling his legends and stories of the old days and the sound of his drum in the wind. And I will always remember what Mishoomis said to me before Mother Earth claimed him...

Nooshehn

As you walk through the bush
    on a summer day
Listen...for nature has sounds;
The sound of leaves and twigs stirring
    under your moccasins,
Thc sound of the wind singing
    through the great trees,
A flock of geese overhead
    beating their wings like heartbeats,
And the songs of my father in your
    heart.
So like the Eagle, stand proud,
For you are my Nooshehn.

ABOUT THE AUTHOR FERGUSON PLAIN

Ferguson Plain, a member of the Bear Clan of the Chippewas, is from the Sarnia Indian Reserve in Sarnia, Ontario. He is a self-taught artist, and all of his works are based on Ojibwa culture. His drawings and paintings combine elements of realism and mysticism. Ferguson now lives in London, Ontario, where he gives workshops on Native culture and is a teacher of Native Education.

children of the World

by Willie Dunn and Guy Trépanier
Illustrated by Luc Melanson

You were born with a dream
And with hope in your eyes
The elders have led
And have bid you to try

Child of waters
Rough with green
Child of the journey
Walk with me

Hold on to your purpose
Hang on to your dreams
Try not to lose direction
Build your self-esteem

Child of talent
Rainbows and trees
Palettes of colors
Of rivers and seas

Seize the tools
That will help you win
Through the culture
That you live within

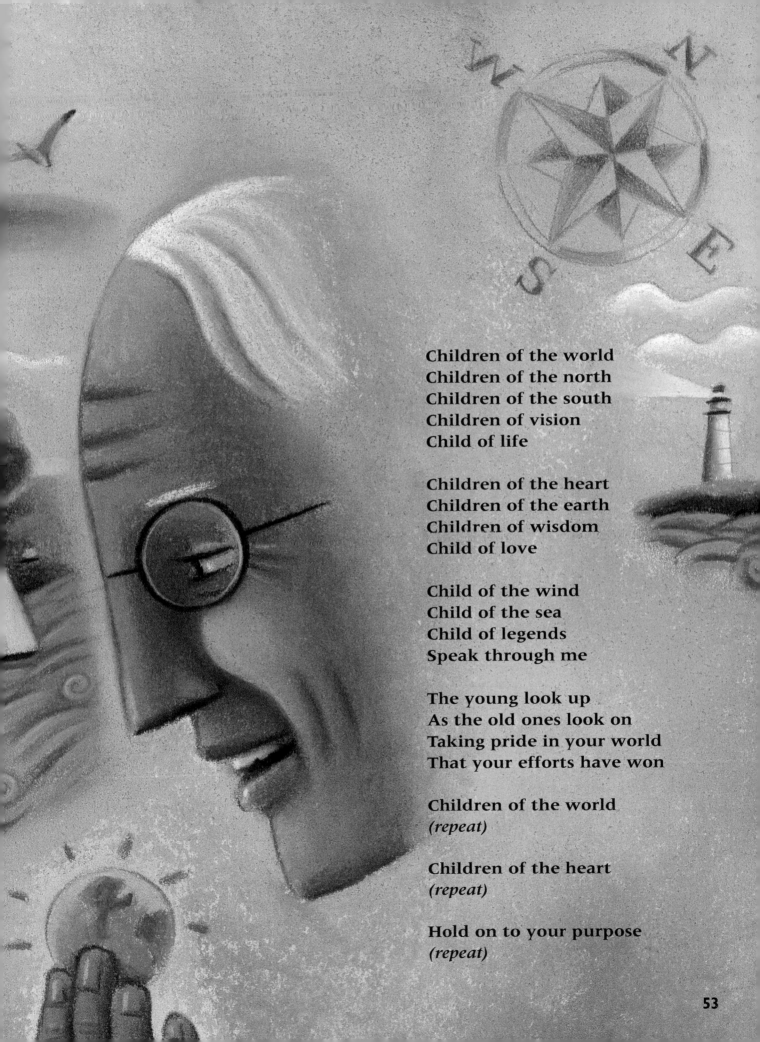

Children of the world
Children of the north
Children of the south
Children of vision
Child of life

Children of the heart
Children of the earth
Children of wisdom
Child of love

Child of the wind
Child of the sea
Child of legends
Speak through me

The young look up
As the old ones look on
Taking pride in your world
That your efforts have won

Children of the world
(repeat)

Children of the heart
(repeat)

Hold on to your purpose
(repeat)

Nathaniel's RAP

by Eloise Greenfield
Photographed by Gilbert Duclos

It's Nathaniel talking
and Nathaniel's me
I'm talking about
My philosophy
About the things I do
And the people I see
All told in the words
Of Nathaniel B. Free
That's me
And I can rap
I can rap
I can rap, rap, rap
Till your earflaps flap
I can talk that talk
Till you go for a walk
I can run it on down
Till you get out of town
I can rap
I can rap
Rested, dressed and feeling
    fine
I've got something on my
    mind
Friends and kin and
    neighborhood
Listen now and listen good
Nathaniel's talking
Nathaniel B. Free

Talking about
My philosophy
Been thinking all day
I got a lot to say
Gotta run it on down
Nathaniel's way
Okay!
I gotta rap
Gotta rap
Gotta rap, rap, rap
Till your earflaps flap
Gotta talk that talk
Till you go for a walk
Gotta run it on down
Till you get out of town
Gotta rap
Gotta rap
Rested, dressed and feeling
    fine
I've got something on my
    mind
Friends and kin and
    neighborhood
Listen now and listen good
I'm gonna rap, hey!
Gonna rap, hey!
Gonna rap, hey!
I'm gonna rap!

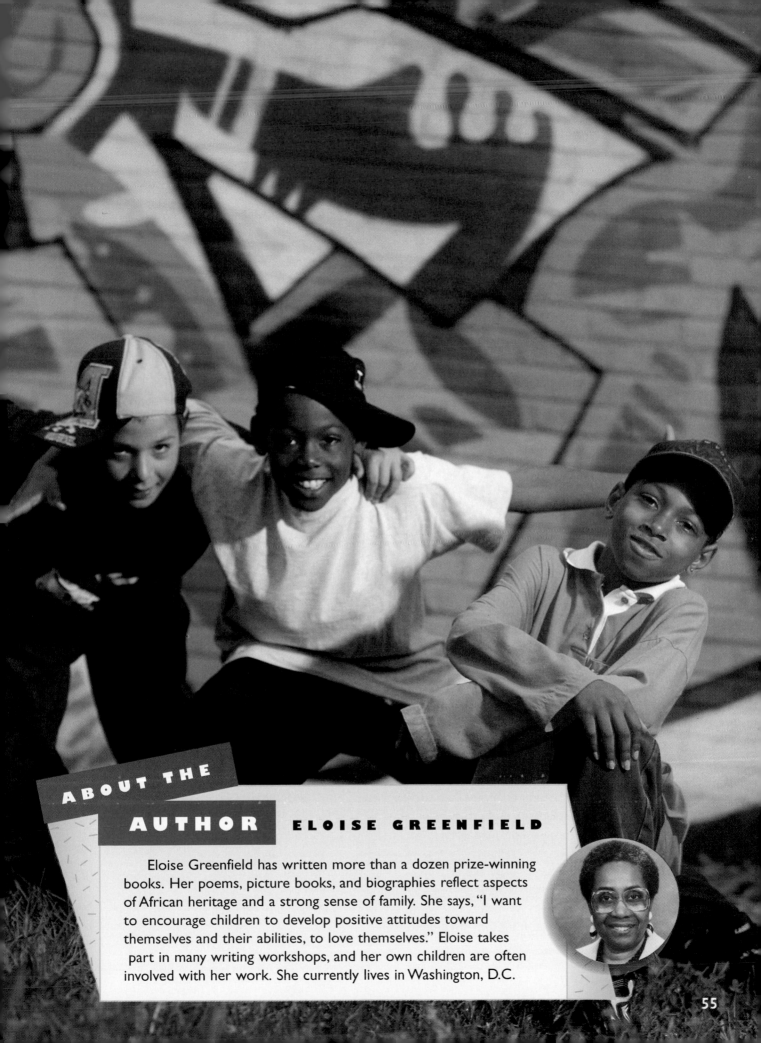

ABOUT THE AUTHOR ELOISE GREENFIELD

Eloise Greenfield has written more than a dozen prize-winning books. Her poems, picture books, and biographies reflect aspects of African heritage and a strong sense of family. She says, "I want to encourage children to develop positive attitudes toward themselves and their abilities, to love themselves." Eloise takes part in many writing workshops, and her own children are often involved with her work. She currently lives in Washington, D.C.

I Love the Look of Words

by Maya Angelou

Illustrated by
Leon Zernitsky

Popcorn leaps, popping from the floor
of a hot black skillet
and into my mouth.
Black words leap,
snapping from the white
page. Rushing into my eyes. Sliding
into my brain which gobbles them
the way my tongue and teeth
chomp the buttered popcorn.

When I have stopped reading,
ideas from the words stay stuck
in my mind, like the sweet
smell of butter perfuming my
fingers long after the popcorn
is finished.

I love the book and the look of words
the weight of ideas that popped into my mind
I love the tracks
of new thinking in my mind.

ABOUT THE AUTHOR

MAYA ANGELOU

Maya Angelou has been an author, poet, journalist, historian, educator, producer, playwright, professional stage performer, and songwriter, and she is presently a college lecturer and instructor! Her many jobs have taken her to countries all over the world, and she speaks six languages. She says, "I believe all things are possible for a human being, and I don't think there's anything in the world I can't do.... All my work is meant to say, 'You may encounter many defeats, but you must not be defeated.'"

WHAT Works BEST for Me

An Open Letter from Richardo Keens-Douglas

Dear Young Readers and Writers,

My name is Richardo Keens-Douglas, and I am a writer. I was born in Grenada. That's an island in the Caribbean Sea. Ever since I was knee-high, I've loved to listen to a good story. In my family, storytelling is a wonderful part of life. On beautiful tropical nights, especially on a full-moon night, we would sit outside on the verandah, overlooking a sparkling moonlit harbor. Somebody would always say, "I remember when..." and right away we would start spinning tales. Sometimes we'd tell folk tales. Or, my father would amuse us with his adventures when he was a young man. My mom would always have a ghost story to tell.

Ever since I was a little boy I've been using my imagination and telling stories. Now I love to write stories, too—magical, adventure, fantasy, comedy, serious, or scary ones. All kinds of stories, for children and adults both. Most of the characters in my stories are Black. The reason is that I feel there is a need for strong Black characters in books for all children. I write my stories for every person in the world to read, though.

One question young readers and writers always ask me is, "Where do you get your ideas from?" Well, my friends, they come to me in all sorts of ways. I could be walking down the street and I might see or hear something that would give me an idea. Or something might happen in another part of the world and a story would come to my mind. Things I've experienced in my own life can spark a story too. Sometimes, though, I just let my imagination run wild, and make up all kinds of fantastic far-out stories.

The wonderful thing about imagination is that there is a wealth of stories hidden inside you. You just have to dig for it. A perfect example is my first children's book, *The Nutmeg Princess*. Besides being a writer, I am also an actor and playwright. I also do lots of school presentations.

One day during one of my presentations, a little Black girl with a Whoopi Goldberg hairdo put her hand up. She said, "Excuse me, sir. Do you know a story about a Black princess?" Right away, my heart sank. I felt very sad, because at that time I didn't know one. This young girl wanted to hear a story about a Princess who looked like her. She wanted all her friends to know that there are Black princesses in magical stories, just like Cinderella and Snow White. So I said to myself, "I will write a story about a Black princess." And that's how *The Nutmeg Princess* came about. The message in that story is, "If you believe in yourself, all things are possible."

So you see, ideas can come to you when you least expect them. You have to remember when you find a good idea, though. So I always carry little blank cards or pieces of paper. Whenever I get a good idea for a story, I jot it down so I don't forget it.

I write mostly at home. Sometimes, on a nice summer day, I take my pencil and writing pad to a cool, quiet spot away from people, and write. I always use a pencil. It's easier to erase when you make a mistake or don't like something. I have no special time to write. It could be late at night, mid-morning, or mid-afternoon.

Writing takes a lot of time and hard work. Each story takes a different length of time to write. It could be one day, or it could be three to six months. Some days I sit down to write a story and absolutely nothing happens. I have an idea, but the story just won't come out of me. I sit for hours, and everything I put on the paper I don't like. When that happens, you know what I always do? I just put the story away and come back to it another day with a fresh mind. Other days, I sit down to write and the story just flows like water from a tap. So the most important thing is to never be discouraged.

For some stories I write, I need to work in complete silence. Other times, I love to put music on. I find it helps me get into the mood. But it must be instrumental music. I remember once I put music on with some guy singing, and when I was finished writing my story I found I had written some of the song words into my story. That's not so good!

I always write in a very particular way. Most of my stories have a storytelling feel to them. You see, I love to write with rhythms and sounds of words. When I am creating a new story, I talk the story out aloud bit by bit first. That's because I need to hear the way the words sound, and the flow of the sentences. Are they short sentences or long sentences? Do the words make you get quiet or sad? Do they make you want to talk out real loud, or maybe sing a line? So I walk around the house talking to myself, repeating certain phrases over and over until the story feels right and sounds right. Then I put it down on paper. That's why I always tell people to have fun reading my stories out loud.

The first and second drafts of my stories are always handwritten. I never use a computer to start creating a story. I always feel rushed with a computer. You know what I mean? I always feel as if the computer is sitting there looking at me with its big square face, saying, "Hurry up and write. I can't sit here all day waiting for your ideas." Ohhhh, I hate that! I like to take my time and enjoy the writing process.

Once a draft is down on paper, *then* the story goes into the computer, where I do all my rewrites and editing. By the way, I never throw away my first handwritten drafts. It's always good to save them just in case you become really famous. In the future, the original handwritten story might be worth something— you never know!

Rewriting can take a very long time or a short time. It all depends on you. When I have finished writing my story, I read it to a couple of good friends whom I trust. Then I perform it in front of different audiences of all ages, to see what works and doesn't work. During this process I do more editing and rewriting.

When I feel the story has all the ingredients a good story would have, I take it to my editor. We sit down and go through the written story to see what works or doesn't work. We check to see if I am repeating myself, or if my sentences are too long. When all of that is done, and we are happy with the finished story, then it goes to be published. And we can all smile. The story is finished.

Now, as I said before, everybody works differently. Sharing my stories with an audience before getting them published is what works best for me. For you, another way may work better. No matter how you work, though, you must love the story you are working on, with all its ups and downs!

Well, my dear friends, I've got to run now. I just got an idea for another story! Remember, never stop reading, writing, and telling stories. I hope to hear from you soon.

Yours truly,

Richardo
Keens-Douglas

Little by Little

by Jean Little
Illustrated by Richard Row

Jean Little, age twelve.

Jean Little was born nearly blind, so it wasn't easy for her to go to a regular school. For one thing, she could only see what was written on the board if she stood with her nose nearly touching it! However, Jean had a gift for words, a talent that would later make her a famous writer. In this episode from her autobiography, Jean discovers the power of words. It happened in 1942....

I was eating my porridge when Hugh fell down the back stairs. Before Mother could get up, he limped in, sniffling slightly, and displayed a bumped elbow for her inspection. Mother examined it gravely.

"A slight haematoma," she said in a serious voice. "And an abrasion almost invisible to the naked eye."

Hugh, who always recovered with the speed of light and who won Mother's admiration with his bravery, chuckled at the impressive words.

"What does that mean?" he asked.

"A little bruise and a scrape I can hardly see."

I glowered at my oatmeal. Why did she have to smile at him like that? He was not so special. I searched my mind for something terrible he had done that I could tell her about.

"Jean, hurry up or you'll be late," Grandma said.

I did not want to go to school. We were going to have another mental arithmetic test. If only I could fall down and break my leg...

Four-year-old Pat grinned at me.

"Huwwy up, Jean," she parroted. "You'll be late."

I wanted to slap the wide smile off her silly little face. Instead I scooped up a few drops of milk on the tip of my spoon and let fly. The tiny bit of milk splashed her on the nose. I laughed. Before anyone could stop her, Pat grabbed up her mug filled to the brim with milk and sent its entire contents sloshing over me, soaking me to the skin.

The next thing I knew, I was back upstairs changing into clean dry clothes. Not only was this going to make me really late, but Mother handed me the knitted suit Aunt Gretta had made for my birthday. Nobody else in Miss Marr's class had a homemade knitted suit anything like it.

"I can't wear it," I said in anguished tones.

"It's lovely," my mother said calmly. "Gretta worked hard to make it for you. Don't be ridiculous. Of course you will wear it."

In ten minutes I was gobbling toast and honey, gulping down milk and hating my cheerful little sister who got to stay home and be spoiled by everybody.

When I reached the street, it was ominously quiet. I really was going to be late, and it was all Pat's fault. I ran the first three blocks, but slowed down when I got a stitch in my side. There was still not a single child in sight.

Then I stood stock still. When I got to school, Miss Marr would tell me to put my name on the board to stay after four. I didn't mind staying late—lots of the others got detentions—I wasn't sure what to write, though I had a strong suspicion that you did not write out your whole name. Did you just write your initials? Or one initial and your surname? Or your first name and your last initial?

I had to get it right. The others still called me names when no teacher was near enough to hear. If I wrote my name up there differently than the others did, they would have a new thing to tease me about. I could hear the jeering voices already.

"You're not just cross-eyed, you're so *dumb* you don't even know how to write your name on the board!"

I stood there, thinking hard. How could I save myself?

I began to walk again, taking my time. I had to invent the most convincing lie of my life. Bit by bit, I worked it out. As I imagined how it must have happened, it grew so real that I began to believe it myself. I had every detail ready as I turned the last corner. Then I began to run.

I knew it was essential that I be out of breath when I arrived.

I dashed up the stairs, puffing hard. I opened the door, said a private prayer for help, and entered the classroom.

"Jean," said my teacher, "you're late."

"Yes," I panted, facing her and opening my eyes wide so that I would look innocent and pitiful. "I know. I couldn't help it."

"Why are you late?" she asked.

I took a deep breath.

"Just as I was going out the door, the telephone rang. You know my mother and father are both doctors and I was afraid it might be an emergency."

Miss Marr opened her mouth to ask a question, but I rushed on.

"The trouble was, you see, that nobody was home but me. So I took the receiver off the hook and I said, 'Dr. Littles' residence.'" Everybody was listening now, even the boys. I kept going.

"MY DAUGHTER IS DYING! MY DAUGHTER IS DYING!"

I saw my teacher jump as I shrieked the words at the top of my lungs. Her eyes were wide with shock. The class gasped. I did not stop for effect. I could not give the teacher time to interrupt.

"It was a man's voice. He sounded frantic with worry. 'I'm sorry,' I told him, 'my parents are out. If you call back, they should be home in one hour.' 'No! Please, don't hang up,' he begged. 'You must come and save her life. If I wait for your parents, she will surely die.' 'Well, I guess if she is dying, I'd better come. Where do you live?' I asked him. '111 King Street,' he told me."

Miss Marr did not even try to ask a question as I paused to catch my breath. The entire class was sitting spellbound. The silence was absolute. Not a desk seat squeaked. Not a giggle broke the hush.

"I hurried in and got the right medicine from the office and then I ran out the door. I didn't go the long way around by the Norwich Street bridge. I was afraid it would take too long. I went down London Road and across some stepping stones down there. When I got to King Street, there was the house. It was a log cabin with wind whistling through the cracks. And as I came up to it, I saw the door was standing open and there were a bunch of people in the doorway and they were all crying. 'What's wrong?' I asked them. 'You are too late,' they sobbed. 'She's dead already.'"

This time, as I snatched a breath, Miss Marr choked back a small sound. She made no attempt to stem the flood of my story. I pressed on.

"'Oh, I am so sorry,' I told them. 'Take me to see her.' So they took me into the cabin and there lay the girl on a trundle bed. Her face was blue and her eyes had rolled up till you could just see white and her teeth were clenched. And her fingers and toes all curled over backwards."

I watched Miss Marr carefully at this point, because I was not absolutely sure what a dead person looked like. The last bit worried me especially. I had heard someone say that when people died, they turned their toes up. That could only mean that their toes curled backwards, but I was not sure about the fingers.

Miss Marr's face quivered a little and her mouth twitched, but she did not speak. I hurried, eager to finish. It would be a relief to sit down.

"'She's not quite dead,' I cried. 'She's just on the point of death. I think I can save her.' I hit her chin and her mouth opened. I poured in the medicine. She fluttered her lashes and turned a normal color and said weakly, 'Where am I?'

I turned and hurried toward the door. But before I could escape, all the weeping people went down on their knees and grabbed hold of my skirt and they said, 'You saved her life! We want to give you a reward. Gold, silver, a bag of emeralds, a horse that will come when you whistle...tell us the one thing you want more than anything else in the world and you can have it.'"

I paused for effect this time. I knew no one would break the hush. I wanted my teacher to take in the next bit.

"'The one thing I want more than anything else in the world,' I told them, 'is to be on time for school.' So they let me go and I ran down the hill and across the stepping stones. When I got to the third last stone, though, I slipped and fell in the river and cut my knee. I had to go home and bandage my knee and put on dry clothes. Then I hurried here as fast as I could. And that is why I am late."

There was a stunned silence in the classroom. Miss Marr

and I stared at each other for a long, long minute. I waited for her to tell me to write my name on the board. Instead she pointed her finger at my desk. Speaking extremely slowly and wearily, she said, "Take...your...seat. Just...take...your...seat."

I tried to keep a solemn expression on my face. But it was hard not to grin. I sat down and did not turn my head as a buzz of whispers broke out behind me. I had missed the mental arithmetic test. I had not had to write my name on the board. And I had kept every single person transfixed with my exciting story.

At least three blissful minutes went by before I realized I had no cut on my knee and no bandage, either. Not only that, but I could not remember whether I had told her which knee I was supposed to have cut.

She had believed me. I was sure of that. Yet any second she was going to discover that I had told her a stupendous lie.

I hooked one knee over the other and clasped my hands around the knee on top. I spent the entire morning that way. When I was required to write, I used only one hand. Miss Marr did not ask me a direct question. When recess time came and she said, "Class, stand," I stayed where I was.

"Jean, aren't you going out for recess?" she asked when the others had marched out and there I still sat.

"Oh, Miss Marr," I said in my smallest, most pathetic voice, "I am so tired from saving that girl's life that I have to stay in and have a rest."

Still clutching my knee with both hands, I laid my head down on my desk and shut my eyes.

She did not say a word.

At noon, when she had her back turned, I ran out of the classroom, dashed home, sneaked Bandaids from my parents' office and plastered them over both knees, to be on the safe side. When I returned to school, Miss Marr smiled and did not ask why both my knees were bandaged.

I sat through the afternoon thinking over what had

happened. Did she really guess? The other kids did not seem to have figured out that I had lied. One girl had even smiled at me, as though she might be my friend. Nobody in my class had called me cross-eyed. A boy in grade seven had, though. If only I could shut him up the way I had hushed everybody that morning.

Then I remembered Hugh's knee. That night I asked Mother, "What are the long words for what's wrong with my eyes?"

I was standing beside her chair. She looked up at me.

"Why?" she asked.

"I want to know, that's all. They call me cross-eyed. I want to know the long words, the ones doctors use."

She rhymed off a whole list.

"Say it again. Slowly."

"Strabismus, nystagmus, corneal opacities, and eccentric pupils."

I practised.

The next day I was late coming out of school. The same

grade-seven boy was waiting for me. He had his first snowball ready.

"Cross-eyed, cross-eyed," he chanted and waited for me to start running so that he could chase me, pelting me with hard-packed snowballs.

I turned on him instead.

"I am not cross-eyed," I said in a strong, clear voice. "I have corneal opacities and eccentric pupils."

I glared at him as I spoke and my eyes were as crossed as ever. But he was so surprised that he stood there, his mouth gaping open like a fish's.

Then I turned my back and walked away. Perhaps his aim was off because he was so used to firing his missiles at a running target. But the first snowball flew past me harmlessly. The second exploded with a smack against a nearby tree.

I kept walking, chin in the air.

In the last two days, I had learned a lot about the power of words. Snowballs would hit me again and I would run away and cry. I would be late and, eventually, I would even have to write my name on the board.

But I had found out what mere words could do. I would not forget.

ABOUT THE AUTHOR JEAN LITTLE

Jean Little was born in Taiwan, where her parents were missionaries. Despite impaired vision, Jean graduated from the University of Toronto and worked as a teacher before becoming an award-winning author. Now almost completely blind, she writes with the aid of a talking computer. In recent years she has combined her writing profession with travel to twenty-nine countries, accompanied by her guide dog, Zephyr. Her books include *Mine for Keeps*, *Mama's Going to Buy You a Mockingbird*, and *Different Dragons*.

Delivering the News

by Linda Granfield
Illustrated by Renée Mansfield

Do you have a paper route? Are there mornings when you don't want to get out of your warm bed to trudge through the cold, dark streets? You probably don't think about how the newspapers in your bundle got there. But all day, and even while you slept, the newspaper's staff worked hard to produce the newspapers for your customers.

Read along and follow the people at the *Clairville Chronicle* as they deliver the news.

11:00 a.m.
Meet and plan

It's a miserable, rainy Monday morning, and people are clutching mugs of steaming coffee as they enter the meeting room. It's time to organize the next day's morning edition of the *Chronicle*. Editors from the various departments of the newspaper sort through information and ideas, and decide what will go into the paper. There are hundreds of possible news items—and not enough space in the paper to print them all.

■ The National editor finds out that the prime minister will make an important speech about national unity.

- The City editor has just picked up a robbery on the police radio.
- The Foreign editor checks the wire service—a volcano is erupting in the South Pacific and lives may be lost.

The most important stories will get the most coverage. Editors debate which stories should make the front page. Some quick decisions have to be made. The more serious stories are called "hard" stories. There'll be room for "soft" stories, too—the visit of Princess Zenobia, the 103rd birthday of Mrs. Elizabeth Hubbard, and an interview with a parrot who reportedly can speak five hundred words. And what's new from the local theatres?

By the end of the morning meeting, the editors have a good idea of what will be going into Tuesday's paper. But more exciting stories can break during the next twelve hours!

Noon
Who's on what?

The reporters and photographers are assigned their stories by the editors. Betty Esposito has been assigned the interview with the talking parrot. She sets up a time and place for the interview, and starts jotting down questions to ask. What *will* she ask a parrot?

Betty will start with the five W's: who, what, where, when, and why. *Who* is the bird—what's her name? *What* kind of bird is she? *Where* did she come from and where does she live now? *When* did she start talking and *why*? Betty will list as many questions as she can. She'll want to do some basic research on parrots. What will get a parrot talking? Maybe she should pack a treat for the bird. How long can she hold the bird's attention? Will she need to wear protective clothing?

With her bag packed full of crackers, pads of paper, and, just in case, a leather glove, **Betty** is off to her interview.

3:30 p.m.
Back at the office

The rain has stopped. The editors are meeting again. Some stories have fallen through. New stories have come up. It's time for some major decision-making and maybe some raised voices.

The News editor is very anxious. Ten stories are competing for front-page coverage. There's only room for six. Marcel Benoit's editor rushes in with the news that the robbery was a non-story.

"But I've got a roof cave-in at Hillside Elementary," he explains.

It's usually the News editor's job to make the final decision about what goes on the front page

and what doesn't. He or she listens while the other editors try to "sell" their stories. Which ones will be chosen? What will best attract and inform the paper's readers? Articles are thrown out and more are selected. The News editor wants a balance of local, national, and international stories—and there are photographs to consider. The News editor makes the front-page selections—but the front page may still change.

6:00 p.m.
Fine-tuning the news

By dinnertime, the front page is ready. Since the afternoon meeting there have been some changes; some of the stories the News editor selected have been bumped off the front page and moved to inside pages. Headlines and leads have been written. Headlines have to grab the reader's attention in a very few words: "Pretty Polly's a vocal bird," "Officials baffled by school cave-in." The lead is the opening to a story and summarizes the whole article.

Throughout the day, stories have been edited and fact-checked. Copy editors check for typos, misspellings, incorrect grammar, and awkward sentences.

START THE TIMER...

Just when Minerva Montez thought her work was done for the day, her editor calls her over.

"Minerva," he says, "Dottie was writing a restaurant review and came down with stomach trouble. She's gone home. We have a hole on page 20, no filler reviews to put in, and guess who's going to write the story?"

He hands over Dottie's notes. Minerva has ten minutes to write the story. How well would you do in her place? Here are Dottie's notes. Set a kitchen timer for ten minutes and start writing!

When you've finished, write a short headline and put your name on the review—that's your *byline*.

TICK TOCK TICK TOCK

Sunday p.m., Minnow's Cafe, Regent Street. Where all the kids hang out, blue walls, yellow cushions, slight smell of what? Chipped plate, had to ask for water, good salad greens, usual veggies, funny waiter Gene, good jokes, seafood in cream sauce, parsley (I hate it), no fork on table, screaming kid in next booth, tables very close, fantastic coffee, dessert (apple pie) so-so, no wine served here, (do waiters deserve tips???), where's my coat, (feeling a bit woozy), waiter found out I was a reviewer, prices high, where are the kids who hang out?

They are on the lookout for anything that might cause legal problems for the newspaper. For example, a newspaper can't accuse a politician of being a thief without proof. Editors also read the stories to see if more information is needed and sometimes jazz up stories to make them more readable—all in an incredibly short time.

A fact-checker may contact story sources to double-check the information in an article. Does Polly speak five hundred words, or is it three hundred? Is Flanagan spelled Flannaghan?

The wire services are checked over and over for late-breaking news that might mean changes for the front page yet again.

Editors decide how much space to fill with their choice of photographs, illustrations, graphs, and maps. Finally, everything is ready to go to the composing room, where the bits and pieces are put together for printing.

The jobs of the editors and reporters are done. Tuesday morning's paper is taken care of, but they must begin to think about Wednesday's paper. Work on a newspaper never stops because the news never stops.

**9:00 p.m.
Getting ready to roll**

Newspaper production constantly benefits from new technology. Not long ago, huge cameras photographed the page layouts, and the negatives of each page were developed in a small darkroom right next to the camera. Now the pages are received by computer as negatives.

These negatives are used to make the printing plates that will go on the press. Each negative is laid on top of the smooth, plastic-coated side of a metal plate. The negative-plate combination is placed in a machine that exposes the negative onto the plate. Another machine washes the plate and removes the unexposed material. (Soon negatives will be obsolete: the page design will be transferred directly onto the plate!)

The finished plate is no longer smooth. If you were to run your fingers over the plastic, you'd feel the bumpy texture of the letters, which are backwards, and the tiny dots of the photos. The finished plate is numbered and sent to the press room, where it will be attached to the press.

9:30 p.m.
Start the presses!

The press room at the *Chronicle* is an im-*press*-ive room about three storeys high. Narrow metal stairs, catwalks, and bridges surround the machinery. Footsteps clang on the metal walkways, the overhead misting machines softly hiss, and the voices of the people running the press rise and fall. Later, when it's time to "roll the presses," the noise will be deafening.

On the floor below the presses are huge rolls of newsprint, some as tall as an adult. As a roll is needed, it is moved into place beneath a press and fed into the machine. The metal printing plates are fixed onto the press and, with the flick of a switch, the paper begins moving through the press in one long sheet at a speed of about 32 km/h.

The printing presses not only print; they also fold and cut the newspapers. The paper is a blur as it moves through the press. Each section of the paper is printed separately, then all the sections meet at the folding machine. The newspapers come off the press with each section in its proper place. Thousands of papers can be printed in one minute. The presses are so noisy that workers have to wear earplugs. Some wear headsets and listen to music.

Some large newspapers, like the *Clairville Chronicle*, print more than one edition a night. The *Chronicle* prints at 9:30, 10:30, and midnight. Sometimes there are only slight changes from one edition to the next. But if an important story breaks, there may be a whole new front page. An editor is usually on hand to deal with any changes. The press can be stopped quickly if major changes are to be made, but such stops can be expensive.

**7:00 a.m.
Tuesday morning**

The news that started its journey at the editors' meeting on Monday has finally arrived for newspaper deliverers, or "newsies," to distribute. When Lindsay Brian does her paper route, she joins a long line of newsies stretching back through more than 100 years of history.

Today, many newspapers still hire boys and girls to deliver papers. But in some communities, parents worry about safety, or kids are too busy for paper routes. So sometimes an adult newsy driving a car filled with newspapers breaks the morning silence, as the *Chronicle* lands on the front porch with a **THUNK**.

ABOUT THE AUTHOR   LINDA GRANFIELD

Linda Granfield, who grew up in Massachusetts, has lived in a suburb of Toronto, Ontario, with her family for the last twenty years. She has written eight non-fiction titles for children and their families, including the award-winning *Cowboy: A Kid's Album*, and *In Flanders Field: The Story of the Poem by John McCrae*. Linda likes to poke around museums, libraries, and dusty second-hand shops, looking for exciting bits of history to research for future books.

Young Authors' Conference

I thought the Young Authors' Conference at our school was fun. It taught me a lot of different things. Peter Eyvindson taught me how to get ideas for stories. Adele Knowler, an artist, showed me how to put lines in the back of my pictures to make them look better. I really liked Kathy Sprenrath, who's a TV reporter, because she taught us how to do news stories. I hope I can go to the Conference again next year.

Marco Derosa
Age 10

I was glad I was picked to go to the Young Authors' Conference and be a part of it. I was interested in the stuff they taught me and I want to learn more about it.

Marco Derosa

How Do You Write a Poem?

```
                     an  idea  I know
               with                   but I
              start                        don't
               to                           have
              says                          one.
            teacher                          I
              My                           search
                                            my
                                           mind,
                                          it's
                                          a
                                       frus-
                                       trating
                                  experi-
                         ence.
                     Nothing,
                      no
                      results.
                      There
                      must
                      be
                      an
                      idea
                  o  m  e
                 s       w
                 •     h
                  e  r  e
```

Kristiann Allen
Grade 4

Peter Eyvindson

Peter Eyvindson is an author who lives in Clavet, Saskatchewan.

Wendy Wolsak is his main artist. I think that she has lots of talent in art and drawing. Peter gets his ideas from his boys Kyle, Konrad, and Kristo, and his wife, Linda. The books that he writes are children's books. These are the books that he wrote: *Kyle's Bath, Chester Bear, Where Are You?, Circus Berserkus, The Wish Wind,* and *Old Enough.* My personal favorite is *Circus Berserkus.* I think it is very funny and comical. I'm sure everybody liked the part when he dressed up like Auntie Monica. That was also funny. Everybody laughed and screamed. I hope that he comes back to Pine Dock someday. I'm sure that everybody else does too!!! He also autographed all the books that he wrote.

Geraldine Simundson
Grade 7

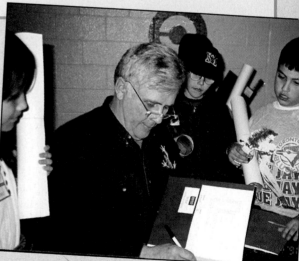

Peter Eyvindson autographing Marco Derosa's book.

Thoughts

Sail away to an adventure
Meet great people
That only lived
In the mind of an author.

See amazing things
never seen,
only
In the written-down thoughts
Of an author.

Alison MacMillan
Grade 6